Grow With Us

The History of Haymarket Baptist Church

For the Quasquicentennial Celebration

Edith Kennedy

Copyright 2019 by Edith Kennedy.

Published 2019.

Printed in the United States of America.

All rights reserved.

No portion of this book may be reproduced, stored in a retrieval system, or transmitted in any form or by any means – electronic, mechanical, photocopy, recording, scanning, or other – except for brief quotations in critical reviews or articles, without the prior written permission of the author.

ISBN 978-1-950647-16-3

Publishng Assistance by BookCrafters, Parker, Colorado.
www.bookcrafters.net

*This history is dedicated to
Andrew Thomas "Tommy" Robinson, Senior,
who, for many years, served Haymarket Baptist
and the people who attended there.
"Roost time, Tommy!"*

Foreword

I AM HUMBLED TO HAVE BEEN OFFERED the opportunity to write the foreword for this historical chronology of Haymarket Baptist Church by Dr. Edith Kennedy, of the birth, growth, transformation, and current prospective years of the church which is located in downtown Haymarket, Virginia on Washington Street. Dr. Kennedy is a superb writer, and she has truly captured the essence of this 125 year-old, vibrant, little place of worship. No matter where you are on your pathway of faith, I believe you will benefit deeply from reading how this little church was born, and how it survived and grew for 125 years. I think you'll find the answer(s) as you read each of the chapters in this publication.

As you may have driven through Haymarket, Virginia, you perhaps wondered about the history of the little, white, pristine church sandwiched between the Haymarket Community Center and the veterinary clinic. If you did, this is the read for you. No boring history here! The church is celebrating its 125th year this year (2019). As you read each chapter in this chronology you will learn many facts and probably a little trivia about a little Baptist Church "that could," and indeed "did"!

My wife and I became members of this congregation

i

about half way through its "transformation" years (chapter 3). I'd like to think we played a small role in its "maintenance" and "stability" during this period, but I don't want to be too presumptuous. During this period the church lost two pastors, another who became the interim pastor later became the full-time pastor for 10 years and then retired. You will read about these servants of the Lord in chapters 3. After a long search for a new pastor, the church ended its transformative years and moved into what is now being referred to as its "prospective " years. These years are going to be very exciting ones! A new pastor, an active youth program, many new, young couples with small children, and a new music director and organist. I will say no more and leave it up to you to discover what is planned for the next 125 years. We hope you will want to become a part of the next century's work for the Lord here at Haymarket Baptist Church. Remember, this is the "little church that could, and, indeed, did! Read on.......

James D. Vail, PhD
Deacon
Associate Dean and Professor, Emeritus, GMU
Colonel, USA (Ret.)

Preface and Acknowledgements

THIS BOOK HAD ITS INCEPTION during the planning stages of the quasquicentennial celebration for Haymarket Baptist Church. To keep you from needing to run for a dictionary, that word means 125th. Previous histories of the church varied in length from a couple of paragraphs to a few pages. In recognition of this anniversary, the planning committee thought they needed a revised history. Little did they know what they were asking for! Dr. Mark Olson asked me if I would be willing to write the history. As I love to research and to write, I agreed. Little did I know what he was asking!

The records of the church were woefully disorganized. Some are missing and some have been destroyed. It took a little over a year to do the research. That included two trips to Richmond, a day spent in the Virginia Baptist Historical Society, personal interviews, and countless hours in the Relic Room of the local library. That does not even take into account the hours, and hours, and hours spent deciphering hand-written notes from meetings. That, of course, could only happen after I found the meeting minutes.

I learned so much about my home church through doing all of this. Much of that could not be shared in this book, but it gives me joy in just the knowing. I hope that you learn something about Haymarket Baptist Church in reading this book and that you will have a greater appreciation of her history and struggles.

I owe thanks to so many people who helped me gather information in preparation for writing this book. To:

> Mark Olson for having confidence in my ability to do this,
>
> The Virginia Baptist Historical Society for preparing the materials for me and for their never-ending patience,
>
> The staff in the Relic Room of the Prince William County Library for helping me locate information, for pointing me in the right direction, and for providing helpful suggestions,
>
> Louise Lightener Jamison for keeping so many mementos,
>
> Ann Whitney for, oh, just for everything,
>
> To those whom I have forgotten,
>
> To all those who didn't run when they saw me coming with more questions.

Our church motto is "Come Grow With Us," thus the title of this book. So, come see how we have grown. And then, come grow with us.

Table of Contents

Chapter 1 Birth..1

Chapter 2 The Formative Years..19

Chapter 3 The Transformative Years....................................41

Chapter 4 The Prospective Years..69

Postscript..77

Appendix A: People who left Antioch Church to start
     Haymarket Baptist Church......................................79

Appendix B: Haymarket Baptist Church
     Property Deed..80

Appendix C: Pastors of Haymarket Baptist Church........81

Appendix D: Baptist Distinctives..82

Photographs..83

About the Author...91

List of Photographs

Long Branch Baptist Church..17
Antioch Baptist Church Original Building......................18
Original Haymarket Baptist Church Building.................35
Washington Street Before 1860...36
Virginia Baptist Orphanage Original Building...............36
Children at Haymarket Baptist Circa 1930......................37
Haymarket Baptist Members 1947....................................38
Original Haymarket Baptist Sanctuary...........................39
Sanctuary After 1973 Renovation......................................40
Sanctuary Following 2012 Renovation.............................67
Burning the Note..68
Haymarket Baptist Church..83
Haymarket Baptist Church July 1984................................84
Old Fellowship Hall prior to last addition......................85
Education Wing Construction..85
Haymarket Baptist Church 2019...86
2019 Kitchen Renovation...87
Haymarket Baptist Church Cemetery...............................88
Garnett Parents Headstone..88
Garnett Children Headstone...88
The Tommy Tree with Tommy Robinson.......................89
The Pastors of Haymarket Baptist Church......................90

Birth
The Family Tree

This is what the LORD says:
Heaven is my throne,
and the earth is my footstool.
Where is the house you will build for me?
Where will my resting place be?
Isaiah 66:1

ON SUNDAY MORNING, Jeffery and Lisa[1] climbed into the back seat of the family van. They whispered quietly but intensely to each other while their mom and dad settled into the front seat.

"But, Lisa!" Jefferey insisted. "You've got to."

"Stop, Jefferey. I don't know! Ask Mom and Dad."

"No way," Jefferey said. "I don't want them to think I don't want to go to church."

"Well I don't know why," Lisa said again.

"But you've got to!"

"I don't know!" Lisa said, raising her voice from the whisper she had been using.

"What don't you know, Lisa?" Mom asked from the front seat.

Silence fell between the brother and sister as they stared at each other. Neither of them wanted to tell their parents what they had been discussing.

"Out with it, you two," Dad chimed in, glancing in the rear-view mirror at his now squirming children.

"Now you've done it," Lisa whispered to Jeffery before answering her mother. "It's Jeffery's question."

"Thanks a lot, Lisa!" Jeffery said.

"So what's the question?" Mom asked.

Jeffery paused a long time before admitting quietly, "I want to know why we go to Haymarket Baptist Church."

"Jeffery!" Mom and Dad exclaimed in unison.

"I thought you understood why it's important to go to church to worship and study about God," Dad said.

"I know that!" Jeffery protested. "I mean why do we go to this church? Why Haymarket Baptist? My friend Matt goes to a Methodist Church."

"And one of my friends goes to a Catholic Church," Lisa added.

"Right, so why Haymarket Baptist?"

"Oh, I see," Mom said, hesitating slightly. "I think we may need to take the long way to church this morning if you want me to answer that question. There's a lot to say."

"I'll drive slowly," Dad said.

"Really slow, Mom chuckled. "Okay, so we go to Haymarket Baptist because . . . "

~~~~~~

Grandmother: Long Branch Baptist Church

IN 1786, THE AMERICAN REVOLUTION had been over for a mere three years, and George Washington had not yet become president. The individual states had each formed their own constitutions before the War ended, but the United States was still operating under the rules of the Articles of Confederation. In 1786 the delegates from five states met in Annapolis, Maryland and called on the Continental Congress to convene a meeting of all state delegates to frame the federal government. It was not until 1789 that the United States Constitution replaced the Articles of Confederation. Despite having no formal government, several treaties were signed with the Indian nations on the east coast. It appeared that a time of peace was beginning for the fledgling country. This provided the opportunity for exploration and experimentation. While James Rumsey tested his first steamboat at Shepherdstown in what is now West Virginia, intrepid explorers pushed further west, expanding the boundaries of the known territory. The United States, with its unique system of government, drew many people seeking freedom.

One such group of people were the Baptists. Many disparate groups of faith systems grew out of the 16th century Protestant Reformation. One of these were the Baptists, so named because they adopted believer's baptism by full immersion. For this practice, they were sometimes referred to as "Dippers." Congregations of people who separated themselves from the national churches of their respective countries were in danger of persecution, imprisonment, or even death. The untamed land of the New World offered these denominations the opportunity to worship as they believed and felt called to do. The first Baptist church in America was established in Providence, Rhode Island in 1638. The First Great Awakening of the 1740s saw tremendous growth in the Baptist denomination. As the time of the Revolutionary War approached, Isaac Backus, a leading Baptist preacher of that era, gave a sermon titled "*An Appeal to the Public for Religious Liberty*" in which he argued for the need of a separation of church and state. His words carried weight, because on January 16, 1786, the General Assembly of Virginia adopted The Virginia Statute for Establishing Religious Freedom and signed it into law three days later. This same concept appeared later in the First Amendment of the United States Constitution which assures that "Congress shall make no law respecting an establishment of religion or prohibiting the free exercise thereof." This promises that the government will not interfere with how a person worships, lives out his or her religious beliefs, or even votes based on those ideals. It was in this atmosphere of purposeful religious freedom that Baptist growth burgeoned.

In 1786, the same year that The Virginia Statute for Establishing Religious Freedom was signed into law, Long Branch Baptist Church[2], with a membership of twenty-five, was constituted under the care of Dr. John Monroe, a physician living in Fauquier County Virginia. As the years passed, numerous pastors were recorded for the church, and membership remained steady. It is reported that in 1810, membership consisted of twenty-six white and twenty-nine colored people. In April of 1817, the congregation, being without a pastor, was then under the leadership of Deacon George Love. It was decided at that time that a new building should be constructed in a more convenient site located approximately a half mile from the original building. After sufficient funds were collected among the members, construction began the following March, and the first service was held in the building in July 1820. This church is located in Halfway, Virginia, so named because it lies halfway between Middleburg and The Plains.

By January of 1928, membership in Long Branch had dropped to five white males, twenty-seven females, and thirty-four colored members. With the arrival of a new minister, William F. Broaddus, membership grew abundantly. In only five years, two hundred people were baptized, and the congregation grew to 128 white and 112 colored members. This sudden growth in Long Branch occurred during a period of religious revival in America known as the Second Great Awakening. Long Branch held firmly to the idea of missionary work that grew out of The General Convention of the Baptist Denominations in the United States for Foreign Missions that met in Philadelphia in May 1914 and undertook to support the work of Adoniram Judson and Luther Rice.

Over the years, Long Branch was a member of four different associations of Baptist churches. It was part of the Ketoctin Association from 1786 to 1820. In 1820, five churches sought release from Ketoctin to form the new Columbia Association, of which Long Branch was a member from 1820 to 1833. The influence of self-named Old School Baptists began to protest the formation of Baptist Associations for the purpose of missionary work and began to exclude some churches who were supporters of unified work. Long Branch was among the group of churches that were barred from the meetings. In 1833, five churches from the Columbia Association withdrew their membership to form the Salem-Union Association. Long Branch was once again among the congregations that formed a new association. Long Branch remained a member of the Salem-Union Association from 1833 to 1856. In 1856, the Salem-Union and Columbia Associations "merged themselves harmoniously and joyfully into the Potomac Association."[3] Though they were members of these different associations, as Haymarket Baptist would be in the future, they held to the Baptist belief that each individual church was autonomous, functioning on its own, not bound by or ruled by another governing body.

The History of Long Branch Baptist Church, in numerous places, details the number of members of both colored and white races. She takes great pride in the fact that "she has always sought the religious welfare of her colored members." This is evidenced by the number of African American members who have attended Long Branch over the years, their attendance sometimes being greater than their white brethren. The church made a concerted effort to provide equality for all her members.

Long Branch Baptist and Haymarket Baptist Have maintained a relationship over the years. In 1974, Rev. Waddell Waters, pastor of Long Branch, was the Revival Speaker at Haymarket Baptist. Rev. Walter Bradley, of Haymarket Baptist, returned the favor and led the revival service at some time in the 1970's. When Haymarket Baptist started a preschool, Long Branch provided scholarships for two students to attend the new school. Rev. Linda Garrett, one of the pastors ordained at Haymarket Baptist, served as pastor of Long Branch at one time. When contacted in reference to this book, the current pastor, Rev. Frank Fishback, willingly provided information about the history of Long Branch.

True to her missionary heritage, Long Branch is the mother church to five local Baptist churches: Mount Hope (1835), Antioch (1837), Middleburg (1847), The Plains First Baptist Church (1872, originally called Cephas Baptist Church) and Marshall (1882). As the mother church of Antioch Baptist, which is the mother church of Haymarket Baptist, this makes Long Branch the grandmother of Haymarket Baptist. The beautiful structure of Long Branch Baptist has been described as one of the loveliest colonial-style churches in Northern Virginia. The members of Haymarket Baptist are thankful for the missional roots from which they spring! Though Long Branch Baptist continues to serve the Lord today, located at 5576 Long Branch Ln., The Plains, Virginia, it is at this point that we must continue to trace the family tree to Antioch Baptist Church.

Mother: Antioch Baptist Church

THE YEAR WAS 1837. It was a time of deceptive calm. The War of 1812 was over, and the Mexican American and Civil Wars were in the future. In that year, the United States recognized The Republic of Texas as a sovereign nation, and Michigan became the twenty-sixth state. On March 1st, 1837, at the age of 28, a young man named Abraham Lincoln was admitted to the Bar Association of Illinois. Yet bubbling just below the surface were signs of impending troubles. In August of 1831, Nat Turner had led a slave revolt that resulted in the deaths of at least 55 people. The tension over slavery would not be quelled for many years. The Battle of the Alamo had been hard fought in 1835. The Panic of 1837 began early in the year, resulting in an economic recession that lasted into the 1940's. William Henry Harrison was inaugurated as president in 1841, and James Marshall's discovery of gold near Sutter's Fort, California elicited the California Gold Rush of 1849. Transcendentalism, the belief that the most important reality is what is sensed or what is intuitive, rather than what is thought, such as scientific knowledge, was taking root in the eastern United States.

Despite the undercurrent of tension, Baptists were busy. In 1837, the American and Foreign Bible Society was formed in Philadelphia by Baptists. Even though traditional Christian beliefs were no longer held in high esteem by the growing numbers of educated Americans, the religious revival of the Second Great Awakening would continue to the middle of the 19th century. While Baptists and Methodists focused mainly on the westward spread of Christianity, growth was also strong in the already settled areas of the United States. Membership in Baptist churches grew rapidly after 1820. The effects of The Second Great Awakening had a lasting impact on America. During that time, social reforms grew, and many new churches were established, with Antioch Baptist Church being one of them.

On April 22, 1837, nineteen members of Long Branch Baptist Church, whose families had moved from Fauquier County to Prince William County near Hopewell Gap, withdrew their membership in order to start a new church closer to where they lived. Though the distance from Halfway to Waterfall, where the new church would eventually be located, was only about four miles, the desire for a new church closer to home was understandable. Roads were typically nothing more than dirt tracks. Melting winter snow and spring rains turned these paths into a morass of mud often a foot deep. In low-lying places, trees were felled and placed across the road. Travel was slow, difficult, and uncomfortable. Many people walked wherever they needed to go. A four-mile trip to church along such roads was not ideal, especially in the cold winter weather. The desire for a new church closer to home was quite understandable and reasonable!

> In the early 1900's, when the young men would take their girlfriends to church Sunday nights (by horse and buggy of course) the men would take a long board with which to bridge the walk from the road to the front door, the mud being a foot deep in bad weather.
>
> Unknown

Not all of the nineteen names of Antioch's founders are known, but some are. John C. Herndon left Long Branch to become pastor of the fledgling Antioch

Church. He was accompanied by George Love and William Broaddus, whose name is prevalent in the historical records of Long Branch. Records do not show how the departing members of Long Branch obtained the property, but they acquired land in Waterfall that had an existing log cabin on it that had once been used as a school. During warm weather, the new congregation of six males and thirteen females met in that building while the church structure was erected. In the colder months, they met for worship and fellowship in homes of the members that would have been kept warm as the unoccupied log cabin would not have been.

Brother Herndon pastored Antioch for only a year before resigning to move to Missouri. A month later, Antioch extended a call to his son, Thaddous Herndon. He accepted and continued as pastor until his death in 1878. The church was without a pastor until 1881 when they secured the services of Brother S. P. Barber. Like his predecessor, he stayed in that position until his death, which occurred in 1882. There followed J. A. Chamblip, Rev. T. P. Warren, G. A. Hall, T. W. Newman, F. P. Barkley, and O. C. Peyton. The last minister that will be mentioned here is Mr. Trainham, who was still serving in 1894. The relevance of this fact and name will be important later.

In 1842, Antioch Baptist Church dedicated its new building and began holding services in the new stone structure. The dedication message delivered by Elder Broaddus was taken from Psalm 102:16. Following the sermon, the business of constituting the church was read and approved by the members. Once the church was duly constituted, they were free to select a pastor. They did this immediately, calling Reverend John C. Herndon, who accepted and immediately began his duties. It is unknown, though likely, that Rev. Herndon would have served more than one church as this was typical at that time.

Two services were held each week at Antioch prior to the Civil War. The Saturday service was for the negro members, and the Sunday service was for the white members. This was a major difference between Antioch Baptist and Long Branch, which had a separate space in the church for African Americans but did allow them to worship at the same time as the white members of the congregation. Few men remained in the area during the years of the Civil War, and services were reduced to once a month, with one pastor serving multiple churches as even the men of God had enlisted on one side or the other of the conflict. Though they served on different sides, they were concerned with ministering to the souls of both Blue and Gray. It was not unusual for a pastor who stayed in the area to serve those at home to travel over 1,000 miles a year on horseback to tend the churches on his circuit.

The area surrounding the church was not spared during the war. Several armies passed through the Hopewell Gap, a narrow pass through the Bull Run Mountains near the church. In the maneuvers leading up to the Second Battle of Manassas, on August 28th, 1862, at the direction of Confederate General James Longstreet, General Cadmus Wilcox led his division through the gap in an effort to outflank Union troops under the command of General James Ricketts. On the trek, Wilcox's troops camped for the night at Antioch Baptist Church. Several weeks later, recovering from a leg amputation, Confederate General Richard Ewell was carried on a litter through Hopewell Gap. Confederate and Union soldiers both lie in the Antioch cemetery, closer in death than they may have been in life.

Though Antioch had suffered through the time of the Civil War, growth in the church blossomed in the years after. Sometime after 1878, the church was renovated, removing the side galleries to accommodate more people. In 1902, with the original stone church no longer meeting the needs of the congregation and in deteriorating condition, it was razed. A new frame building was erected on the site of the first structure. During construction of the new building, Sunday School and worship services were once again held in the log cabin where the church had first met. In 1909, Antioch Baptist joined the Potomac Baptist Association, in which Long Branch Baptist was a member.

As with Long Branch, Antioch Baptist and Haymarket Baptist have maintained close ties through the years. They have shared pastors and, sometimes, even members. Revivals and homecomings at the two churches have drawn visitors from both congregations. Family ties are hard to break!

Daughter: Haymarket Baptist Church

HISTORY REALLY DOES REPEAT ITSELF. In 1894, 28 people, with the blessing of Antioch Church, withdrew their membership from that congregation to start a new church closer to where they now lived. Like mother, like daughter! The names of those departing from Antioch read like a who's who of that membership[4] and the prevalent residents of Haymarket. They would bring the same religious zeal and love of God to the new church as they had to the mother church.

The location for the new church was near the center of Haymarket, Virginia, a small town in northwest Prince William county. The town has been known by many names: The Crossroads, a name which was derived from the many hunting trails traversed by Native Americans; Red House, so named for the ordinary of the same name situated at the intersection of the Carolina Road (now Old Carolina Road) and the Gap Road (now Washington Street or Route 55); Skinkerville after William Skinker who owned the land on which the town was built and who laid out the original town plan; and finally, Hay Market, which was eventually shortened to Haymarket in 1838. The origin of that name is debated. Some believe that it is due to the racetrack that once operated in the town, beginning where Tyler School now stands and ending behind Haymarket Baptist Church. The local interest in horses for racing and foxhunting created a thriving hay market in the town. Others assert that it derived from the Hay Market Inn, which was named for the family seat of the Skinkers in England. When William Skinker solicited the General Assembly of Richmond in 1798, he applied for a town to be established and called Skinkerville. In 1799 the Assembly responded that the town of Hay Market be stablished. It is not known why the Assembly rejected

Skinkerville and established Haymarket, but many are happy with that decision!

During the Civil war, both Confederate and Rebel troops traveled through the town because of the converging roads. On the night of November 5th, 1862, Federal troops set the town on fire in retaliation for Confederate troops capturing supply wagons and killing Union soldiers standing guard. Only three houses and the walls of St. Paul's church survived the blaze. Red House Ordinary was destroyed at that time but was later rebuilt. It is now a thriving retail and office space in Haymarket. Recovery after the fire was difficult, but the residents were determined to save their town. Slowly the town was reconstructed, and it was into this small but geographically important area that the new Haymarket Baptist Church would be built.

~~~~~~

"Wow, Mom! How do you know all that stuff?" Lisa asked.

"Because somebody wrote a book about it," Mom said. "And I read it."

"But, Mom," Jeffery protested. "All that was interesting, but you still haven't explained why we attend this church. Why Haymarket Baptist Church?"

"I did just tell you three of the reasons," Mom said.

"Well, I didn't get it," Jeffery answered.

"The reason that we go to a Baptist Church has to do with what makes a Baptist church Baptist. They're called Baptist Distinctives. There are several of these, but the three I've already mentioned are the belief in baptism of only adults by full immersion, the belief that the people of the church own and are responsible for the maintenance and the running of the church, and that Baptist churches are autonomous."

"Autono . . . what?" Jeffery asked.

"But Kate was baptized last week, and she's not an adult," Lisa added.

"But she's old enough to make the decision herself. It isn't something that her parents had done to her," Dad explained.

"Oh, I see. So what about the other thing? That autono whatever," Jeffery prodded.

"That just means that Baptist churches are independent. They join together to accomplish things, like mission work, but they are not under the control of a governing body," Mom explained. "Each church is free to do what it wants."

"And do we really own the church?" Lisa asked.

"Yes," Dad said before Mom could answer. "In a sense. It's really God's church, but the people who attend Haymarket Baptist church make the decisions about what is to be done, how the money is spent, and who to hire. That's why we have business meetings where everything is voted on by the members of the church."

"That's why those 28 people could leave Antioch Baptist and start a new church all on their own. It was their decision and would be their church," Mom explained.

"Okay. I get that part. We like Baptist churches. But why this particular Baptist church?" Lisa asked.

"Right!" Jeffery said. "There are other Baptist churches

around. And it's not like we have to drive through mud that's a foot deep to get there."

"Yeah. So why Haymarket Baptist Church out of all the others around?" Lisa asked.

"Do you really want to know more?" Mom asked in surprise.

~~~~~~

Chapter Notes

1. Jefferey and Lisa are the fictitious characters of the Children's Sermon at Haymarket Baptist Church
2. Information about Long Branch Baptist Church is taken from John K. Gott, ed., *History of Long Branch Baptist Church, Fauquier County, Virginia: 1786-1967* (1967).
3. The Potomac Association would later change its name to NorthStar Network of Churches, of which Haymarket Baptist is now a member.
4. See Appendix A for a list of the founding members of Haymarket Baptist Church.

Long Branch Baptist Church

Original Antioch Baptist Church Building

The Formative Years

There is a time for everything,
and a season for every activity under the heavens:
a time to be born and a time to die,
a time to plant and a time to uproot
Ecclesiastes 3:1-2

"Yes!" Jefferey and Lisa said in unison.

"Okay. So far you've met the grandmother and the mother churches. Now let's take a look at this church in more detail.

"Good!" Jeffery exclaimed.

"How much are you going to tell us?" Lisa asked in a worried voice.

"Just enough so that you understand why we chose this church to attend," Mom said. "Not a lot," she added reassuringly.

"Okay, go ahead," Jeffery said.

~~~~~~

The writings of Wirt Trainham, the first pastor of Haymarket Baptist Church, indicate that, under his leadership in recognizing the need for a church in "the village of Haymarket," Haymarket Baptist was organized on October 22, 1894. The 28 members who left Antioch Church to start a new Baptist Church wasted no time in getting organized. On November 1st, 1894, the newly selected trustees, George H. Smith[1], William W. Jordan, and T. E. Garnett, entered into an agreement with George H. and Mildred J. Smith, G. M. White, and R. L. Payne to purchase land "on the North side of the Gainesville road and running 34 1/2° E. 9 Poles to Stake No. 2. thence 55 1/2° W 5 Poles to Stake No. 3. thence S. 34 1/2° W 9 poles to Stake No. 4. Thence S. 55 1/2° E 5 Poles to the beginning and containing 45.9 square poles of land."[2] This land acquisition equaled about .28917 acre and was sold for the grand sum of ten dollars! The deed stipulated that the named trustees and their successors were to hold "said land in trust for the erection thereon of a Baptist Church building and necessary appurtenances, and for no other purpose whatever." Haymarket Baptist owned land!

It is important to take note of the names of the people involved in this transaction. The list of people who left Antioch on this new venture contains the name George H. Smith; this is probably the same as the George W. Smith whose name appears on the deed for the property. The handwriting of that time is often difficult to decipher. (See Endnote 1 for more information regarding this.) Also on that list are Mildred Smith and W. W. Jordan. Mr. and Mrs. Smith were both sellers and receivers of the land! They were obviously totally committed to the starting of a new church in Haymarket. It is also noteworthy that the name Hulfish appears four times on the list of those who obligated themselves to start a new church. The Hulfish family was prominent in the town of Haymarket at that time. Other names on that list are well known in the area to this time.

Between the time of the initial organization of Haymarket Baptist and the completion of the building, the congregation met in the Haymarket Town Hall. It seems that in a very short time, membership began to grow. This is evidenced by the fact that at least some of the names of Trustees were not on the list of those who first started the church.

There is no historical record of when construction on the new church began, but it was completed sometime in 1895. The original building consisted of just the sanctuary. Many recollections claim that the original building also had two small classrooms and a baptistry. However, research has brought evidence to light that these were actually additions that will be discussed later. Sunday School classes in the new church would have been held in various areas of the sanctuary. Wherever these were held, the church was reaching people for God. The first baptisms were recorded on May 19th, 1895 when Lawrence Hulfish and Charles Jordan became the first congregants to undergo this ordinance in the new church. This was probably done in the North Branch Creek, located across the road from the church.

Light in the sanctuary of the building was provided by candles, and heat was from a pot-bellied stove located in what is now the choir loft. On windy days, the smoke from the stove would blow back into the sanctuary, causing the congregation to cough, and almost obscuring the pastor! These were dedicated people who endured this to worship their Lord and Savior.

On August 14th, 1895, Haymarket Baptist Church applied for and received unanimous admission to Potomac Baptist Association at the annual meeting held at Belle Air Church in Stafford. At that same meeting, Rev. Trainham delivered the report on education. Haymarket Baptist was now a fully accepted church and welcomed into the same flock as Long Branch and Antioch on equal footing.

Not all was happy for the fledging congregation, however. Graves located on church property record the deaths of the Garnett family. Two children, Mabel, born in 1885, and Robert, born in 1887, died on March 15th and March 14th, 1896, respectively. Their graves are marked with the words "The Lord Gives and the Lord Hath Taken." The children were followed in death by their parents, Thomas E. in 1922, and Molly B. Garnett in 1949. The children were victims of pneumonia. At that time, as it is even today, pneumonia was deadly. It was the third leading cause of death in the late 1800's. It must have been devastating for this family to lose their children so close together! It is interesting to note that T. E. Garnett was one of the Trustees named in the deed for the property on which the church rests.

The Haymarket Baptist Church building was dedicated on August 30, 1896. At that time, Rev. Trainham was pastor of the field of churches consisting of Haymarket Baptist, Antioch, Little River, and Manassas Baptist. Reverend Trainham was reported to be a great man of God. His works certainly demonstrated that. It has already been mentioned that he pastored numerous churches in the northern Virginia area. He also served in Southwest Virginia at Marion and at the Bruington and St. Stephen's churches in King and Queen County. After pastoring at these churches, he returned to this area and served as the first associational missionary for the Potomac Association. During that time, he traveled throughout Fauquier, Fairfax, Prince William, and Loudon counties, visiting and speaking at different churches.

> Baptists do not base their appeal upon the remoteness of their origin, the continuity of their existence, the measure of their success, nor the largeness of their numbers, but rather upon the closeness of their adherence in faith and practice to the teachings of the New testament. By this we would be accepted or discredited.
>
> Wirt Trainham

From 1904, when Rev. Trainham left the area, to 1962, Haymarket Baptist was pastored by eleven different men. No information is known about these servants of God except that they worked very hard for very little earthly reward. At that time in American history, churches did not employ full-time pastors. Instead, one man would lead several churches, with services held only on certain Sundays of the month at the various churches. These meetings were optimally held bimonthly, but sometimes less often than that. If churches were in close proximity so that travel time was not onerous, worship services were held prior to the Sunday School hour at one church in order to accommodate the pastor being able to preach at a second location later the same day. It may seem that eleven pastors in only 58 years is a high rate of turnover. Only two pastors, Council and Taylor, reached into the double digits of employment. The others, after accounting for times when the church was without a pastor, averaged only three years each. This high rate of turnover could be attributed to the rigors of traveling between different churches with disparate congregations.

Another consideration was the rate of pay. The earliest financial records from Haymarket Baptist Church, from the year 1916, indicate that the pastor was paid a whopping yearly salary of $100 for typically bimonthly preaching. This payment was not indicated as part of the budget of the church, so it must have been collected from the members for the purpose of paying the pastor. Records for 1916 show that there were 37 members in the church with expenditures of $54.15 to pay the staff, indicated as for music. Income for that year was $45.32, leaving a shortfall of $8.83. It seems that budget issues are nothing new for churches!

In 1917, the pastor's salary was raised to $150 annually. In addition to this increase, Haymarket Baptist was already beginning to reach outside of itself to help spread the gospel to other places and people. Budget notations for that year show that money was sent to support both home and foreign missions. The Southern Baptist Convention had been formed in May of 1845, and Haymarket was already participating in that far reaching missions effort. In April of 1917, Haymarket Baptist also sent money to the Baptist Orphanage of Virginia. This organization was founded in 1890. Its original mission was dedicated to serving the needs of orphans, but during the years of the

Great Depression, many families simply could not take care of their children. These children also found a home at the Baptist Orphanage of Virginia. As the economy improved following World War II and the needs of society and children changed, the Orphanage altered its mission to focus on children who were at risk because of abuse or neglect. We now know this institution as HopeTree Family Services, and Haymarket Baptist Church still supports it in its effort to minister to children, youth, and developmentally disabled adults.

By 1918, membership had grown to 76 members, but took a dip to 69 in 1919. However, by 1923, membership had grown to 81! The young church was now 29 years old. It was already moving toward the church it would become, growing its members, helping to spread the gospel throughout the United States and the world, and helping the less fortunate.

A newspaper article dated March 3, 1923 states that "An addition of two Sunday School rooms and a baptistry is being added to the Haymarket Baptist Church." Despite the recollections mentioned previously, this is when the baptistry and the two rooms were built. The baptismal pool was located at the rear of the pulpit area and was flanked on each side by a door that led to the new Sunday School rooms. The rooms were equipped with wood burning stoves and tables that were hinged to the wall. When needed, the legs were extended and the tables were lowered to the floor. When classes were over, the tables were lifted and secured to the wall, conveniently out of the way. There was no waste of space there! Adult classes were still held in different parts of the sanctuary. A visit to

Haymarket Baptist today will surprise most people at just how small those first Sunday School rooms were!

Even at that time, Haymarket Baptist was a forward-thinking church. Most congregations of that period performed baptisms in a nearby creek, sometimes needing to dam the flow of water to create a deep enough pool for the complete immersion required by Baptists. Haymarket Baptist, however, now had an indoor baptistry. To fill the baptistry, water was collected from the run-off of the roof, a modern idea for saving water today, or hauled from North Branch Creek. The water was heated by building a fire in the church yard and heating railroad irons that were then submerged in the baptistry pool.

The future looked bright for Haymarket Baptist! In 1954, the church received its first addition of land. This was donated by Mr. and Mrs. Charles Gillis. In 1956, more land was donated by Robert L. Fletcher in memory of his wife Elsie Lambert Fletcher. Located outside of the town of Haymarket along Rt. 55, this land was to be used for a parsonage. Most of the construction of the house was done by members. Rev. Edward H. Clarkson (1956-1960) and his family were the first residents. Russell O. Cutchins (1962-1967) was the first full-time pastor called by Haymarket Baptist. As with the other early pastors, very little is known about him. He was born April 3, 1930 in Newport News, VA to parents Wesley Ocie Cutchins and Joyce Edwards Cutchins. Rev. Cutchins pastored several churches in addition to Haymarket Baptist, including Connarista Baptist Church in Aulander, N.C. and Bethlehem Baptist Church in Richmond, VA. He was a member of the Golden Notes Senior Choir in Bon Air,

VA and was an advocate for the disabled in Virginia. Rev. Russell Owen Cutchins passed into heaven on Aug. 28, 2014 at the age of 84.

Though little is known of Rev. Cutchins, during his tenure at Haymarket Baptist, the church itself went through its first transformation. The church that was listed in the 1939 Potomac Association annual report as having four rooms was growing, so much so that the membership no longer had enough space in those four rooms to conduct God's work. (It isn't clear what the fourth room was as reported by Potomac Association. Records indicate only three rooms at that time.) To accommodate the need for additional classroom space, a first floor Educational Building was added. This project was financed through the bank and work was done by a construction firm owned by a member. This addition was designed with the intention of adding a second floor in the future to meet the anticipated membership growth. This first structural addition was dedicated in 1960.

> The bell in the steeple was always rung on Sunday mornings to let people know it was church time. It was such a pleasant sound to hear on Sunday. At home we could hear the church bell ringing. As I reminisce, I am forever grateful for the many wonderful experiences and opportunities that I received from Haymarket Baptist Church.
>
> Louise Lightner Jamison

In February of 1964, a special planning committee was proposed and accepted by the members of Haymarket Baptist. The purpose of this committee was to investigate long-range plans for church growth and expansion. They were to formulate a plan for additions to the building to meet the needs of the growing membership in the church. Another addition of one acre of land was given to Haymarket Baptist by Breckenridge Rust, a nephew of Mr. and Mrs. Charles Gillis, who had previously donated land to the church. This gift was given in their memory in June 1964. Another area of growth in the church was the start of Sunday evening services. The church that began with only 28 members had come a long way from the time that they held services on an irregular bimonthly schedule. Now they had services twice on one day!

The Planning Committee that had been instituted in February was ready by May to give their study results. It was time to add that second floor! They recommended that a Building Committee be formed to handle the business of the new addition. Construction on the second floor of the Educational Building was again financed through a local bank. Construction was contracted to a local builder. This second addition was completed, and the final payment to the contractor was made in February of 1965. The dedication for the new Education area was held April 25, 1965. For those of us who are math challenged, that is only five years between these two additions!

The year 1966 marked more milestones for Haymarket Baptist. Membership had grown to 190, and the annual budget was now $17,406. Antioch Baptist, with a declining membership and only 7 or 8 people attending regularly, officially closed. The members were released to relocate to a church of their choice. Most of them joined Haymarket Baptist. Haymarket Baptist was also made the trustee of the funds left in the Antioch bank account and of the property where the church was located. Their brass communion set was also sent to Haymarket Baptist. In November 1966, Wilhelmina Rust donated a 20-foot right-of-way giving access to the acre of land behind the church.

Just as Haymarket Baptist was progressive in having an indoor baptistry, it was also on the cutting edge of the Civil Rights Movement. While many churches at that time denied admittance to Negroes, in 1966, Haymarket Baptist Deacons simply stated that issue was covered in the Church Constitution Article II Section 3, which at that time read membership was by one of two methods: "By Baptism: Any person professing faith in the Lord Jesus Christ may be received as a candidate for baptism" or "By Letter: Upon presentation of, pending receipt of, a letter, members of other Baptist Churches of like faith may be received." The Deacons accepted the statement that "any person professing Faith in the Lord Jesus Christ" included all races. Everyone was eligible for membership in Haymarket Baptist Church.

The new year of 1967 brought even more changes. The first telephone was installed in the church. There was an $8 installation fee, and the monthly bill was $7.75. This year also saw the start of radio broadcasts of the Sunday morning service. The Church members voted to purchase an old school bus that would be used to pick up children from the surrounding neighborhoods and bring them to church on Sunday morning. In June, Rev. Cutchins announced that he was resigning as pastor. The following month, Rev. Walter Bradley was called as the new minister.

There was a huge expansion of programs under the

leadership of Rev. Bradley and his wife Kathryn. Rev. Bradley was a graduate of the University of Richmond with a degree in Political Science and from Union Theological Seminary with a Bachelor of Divinity. The Bachelor of Divinity at that time is equivalent to the current Master's Degree of Divinity. Mrs. Bradley held a degree in voice from Averett Junior College[3] and went on to Southern Baptist Theological Seminary to earn a Bachelor of Sacred Music as a voice major.

Radio broadcasts continued, and the Bradleys began Sunday morning worship services at Silver Lake Campground in 1968. There was a music program already established at Haymarket Baptist, but when that family moved away, Mrs. Bradley began working with the choir. Under her guidance, Haymarket had a Men's Choir, Lady's Choir, Youth Choir, Children's Choir, and Adult Choir. This was in addition to voice lessons offered to choir members free of charge and singing at other church revivals and programs. Rev. Bradley also started the Haymarket Herald, the church newsletter. This is still printed today, though the format has changed. The original Haymarket Heralds were one page, front only, so that it could be folded in half and mailed to members.

In March of 1968, a short three years since the dedication of the second floor Education rooms, a new planning committee was formed to study the need for a third addition of classrooms. There had been a great deal of growth in the Sunday School, possibly due to the purchase of a second bus to bring children to church on Sunday morning. It was debated whether to add a third floor to the existing rooms or to expand outward. In 1969, the plans were accepted for a new two-story addition. In 1970, the third addition, consisting of two floors, was dedicated debt-free through a special membership offering. The design of this addition was drawn by a church member, Oscar Burdett, and the work was performed by the church family. This addition came just in time because it was reported in the Deacon meetings that the Primary Sunday School department was over-crowded. An enrollment goal of 220 in Sunday School was set for 1973. It is not recorded whether that goal was met or how close the number may have come. But the concept of setting such a number indicates that it was seen as a possible achievement. Sunday School was thriving!

In 1973, again using plans drawn by Oscar Burdett, the sanctuary was renovated for the first time. The pulpit area was raised to make the speaker more visible and the choir and piano areas were switched. Perhaps most welcome of all, the sanctuary was carpeted, and padded pews replaced the old wooden ones. The original pulpit furnishings and two pews now grace the Sunday School entrance of the present church building. The church members contributed offerings to finance this renovation, also done debt free, and most of the work they completed themselves. The building fund goal of $10,000 was met and surpassed. Due to these renovations, the Haymarket Baptist Church sanctuary was removed from the Prince William County Historical Record.

The purchase of property adjoining the parsonage was completed in 1975. The kitchen was renovated in 1976. Also in 1976, Services began at Hillwood Trailer Court in Gainesville. This meant that Rev. Bradley presented three services each Sunday Morning: Silver Lake, Hillwood Trailer Court, and Haymarket Baptist. He also led the Wednesday night Bible Study and Prayer meeting. The Youth of the Church led the Sunday evening services, which were followed by their choir practice. The other adult choirs met following Prayer Meeting on Wednesday, and the children's choirs rehearsed prior to Prayer Meeting. In 1982, Haymarket Baptist began recording the Sunday morning worship service so that shut-ins could have a copy of it to listen to.

Unfortunately, everything was not happy at Haymarket Baptist. Several new families had transferred their membership to Haymarket Baptist during the 1970's and 1980's. They were not satisfied with the work that Rev. Bradley was doing. They drew some other members into this disagreement, giving the reason for their discontent that Rev. Bradley was not doing enough at the church and was too involved in affairs of Potomac Association. It is true that the Bradleys took part in Associational events, and the Annual meeting was held at Haymarket Baptist in 1972. Rev. Bradley presented the sermon, Mrs. Bradley performed the special music, and the Haymarket Baptist Youth Choir, under the direction of Mrs. Bradley, also presented special music. Despite his involvement with Potomac Association, Rev. Bradley was extremely busy in the church as evidenced by the number of services he led each week. In addition to these, he also visited with sick members, went to see visitors, attended committee meetings, and conducted weddings and funerals. During his time at Haymarket Baptist, average attendance at Sunday morning worship was 150 with 180 in Sunday School. Mrs. Bradley led the numerous choirs, all without pay.

Despite the loyalty of many members, those who were not satisfied were quite vocal. The church was slowly forming into two factions. To prevent any further damage to the church he loved, Rev. Bradley retired from Haymarket Baptist in 1983. One side felt victorious and was quite happy with the result they had achieved. The other side, which consisted of long-time members, was saddened by the turn of events in their church. This was the first schism to rock Haymarket Baptist Church. But it was nothing compared to what was to come.

~~~~~~

"OH NO! DID THAT REALLY HAPPEN? At our church?" Lisa asked sadly.

"I'm afraid so," Mom said.

"But what are we supposed to learn from this?" Jeffery asked. "What does this tell us about Baptist churches and why we attend one?"

"Remember I said that the members run the church and make the decisions?" Mom asked.

"Yes," Jeffery and Lisa said together.

"Sometimes the decisions aren't good. Sometimes people get hurt. But we also talked about Baptists believing that the Bible is absolutely true."

"Right," Jeffery answered. "Rev. Trainham said that."

"Well I hope there's some good news after this," Lisa said.

"Then are you ready for the next chapter?" Mom asked.

"Yes," Lisa said. "Tell us something happy."

~~~~~~

Chapter Notes

1. The initials for this name are a best guess as the handwriting was difficult to decipher. No printed version was available.
2. From Haymarket Baptist Church deed. See Appendix B
3. Averett Junior College is now Averett University.

Original Haymarket Baptist Church Building

Washington Street before 1860

Virginia Baptist Orphanage Original Building

Children at Haymarket Baptist - Circa 1930

Haymarket Baptist Members - 1947

Original Haymarket Baptist Sanctuary

Sanctuary after 1973 Renovation

The Transformative Years

*Where there is no revelation, people cast off restraint;
but blessed is the one who heeds wisdom's instruction.*
Proverbs 29:18

"SO WHAT HAPPENED NEXT?" Jeffery prodded.

"Did things get better?" Lisa asked.

"Yes, things got better," Mom said reassuringly.

"Yeah, before they got even worse," Dad said ominously.

~~~~~~

GOD BLESSED HAYMARKET BAPTIST with the presence of Dr. Bruce Miller, who served as the interim pastor following the forced retirement of Rev. Bradley. Dr. Miller had earned both Bachelor's and Master's degrees from Baylor University where he carried dual majors in religion, philosophy, English/speech, and applied violin. He went on to earn a Ph.D. in Philosophy from the University of Southern California, where he also served as chaplain. Dr. Miller combined his knowledge of Philosophy and Religion into a healing presence that helped to salve the wounds of Haymarket Baptist Church. In his book,

Ideology and Moral Philosophy, Dr. Miller wrote that moral ideology, as opposed to an immoral ideology that seemed to be threatening society, was a balance between three things: a world view which synthesizes knowing and believing; a dynamic which synthesizes believing and doing; and a methodology, which synthesizes doing and knowing. It was this philosophy that he brought to the people of Haymarket Baptist in its hour of need.

As can be imagined, the change from Rev. Bradley to a pastor who held a doctoral degree and could invent the ideas just mentioned was a huge shift for the wounded church. This was the first pastor with a doctorate that Haymarket Baptist had ever employed. It was a definite change, but one that helped the people to heal. There were some members who, from the outset, did not believe that such a man as Dr. Miller could serve a church like Haymarket Baptist. There was almost an aura of distrust for a man who was so well educated. What could he possibly teach that would be of benefit to a rural church?

What Dr. Miller taught was the same as what he had written. Believers must first have a world view that was a full measure of both believing and knowing. These two may sound like the same thing, but they are actually different. A person can believe that the sun will rise tomorrow. But knowing that the sun will rise tomorrow takes that belief one step further; there is absolute assurance in knowing. In much the same way, a person can believe that Jesus is the risen Son of God. Knowing that is the assurance that it is absolutely true. Added to this is the element of doing. Belief and knowing are hollow if those dogmas are not put into action. That action then leads to a deeper *knowing*. Through his words and, more importantly, through his actions and presence, Dr. Miller led the people of Haymarket Baptist forward out of the hurt that had enveloped them. It did not take long for those members who had doubted him to realize that Dr. Miller could be and was a definite benefit to Haymarket Baptist and to God's Kingdom.

Dr. Miller's days at Haymarket Baptist were filled with spending time with those who were ailing, and with helping the deacons to function as effective spiritual lay leaders of the church. He traveled with the deacons to Eagle Eyrie[1] for spiritual retreats that left them refreshed and renewed. He also taught small group studies that were spiritually based but functioned to lead participants to a deeper understanding of service to God, the epitome of the synthesis of doing and knowing. One of his greatest gifts to Haymarket Baptist Church was his admonition to not take his word for what the Bible said. He charged everyone to "check for yourself to be sure I'm right." In this way he led members to dig deeper into the scriptures.

Even though Dr. Miller held several degrees, he never put himself above the members of Haymarket Baptist Church. He encouraged and gently pushed the congregation to take seriously the Baptist tenant of the Priesthood of the Believer. This idea comes directly from New Testament passages that teach that all believers have access to God without the intervention of a priest *or pastor*. Dr. Miller led his congregation to accept responsibility for themselves in their beliefs. By gently urging, Dr. Miller encouraged the people of Haymarket Baptist through a very difficult time in the church's history. While members could have focused on what had been and what had happened, Dr. Miller gave them a new focus on what could be. Through his guidance and leadership, Haymarket Baptist began once again to work together as a united church body.

Haymarket Baptist was on the way to healing. Dr. Miller had guided the church so well that many members wanted him to become the new permanent pastor. However, Dr. Miller did not believe that an interim pastor who served a church during a crisis should then become its full-time pastor. He thought that such an action could actually prolong the healing that had already started. He declined the offer to stay at Haymarket Baptist. In April of 1983, Haymarket Baptist Church called Rev. Larry L. Lee to be its fifteenth pastor.

Rev. Lee held a Bachelor of Theology from Piedmont Baptist University, a Bachelor of Arts from Averett University, and a Master of Divinity from Southeastern Baptist Theological Seminary. While serving as pastor at Haymarket Baptist, he was working on a Doctor of Ministry from Wesley Theological Seminary. As with most pastors, Rev. Lee brought changes. In 1984, the church hired a Summer Youth Leader. Edith Kennedy was the first person to fill this position but was followed by many others. Enrollment in Sunday School and attendance

> I remember VBS and being in the 5th grade learning the books of the Bible in order from my Grammie and what the different sections were. No one teaches that anymore
>
> Becca Wholgemuth

for worship service was still strong. In anticipation of expected increases in enrollment due to the development of the area around the church, in 1986, another addition was added to Haymarket Baptist. This consisted of a large fellowship hall and two wings of classrooms. This was the first time that the church went so deeply into debt for an addition to the building. The trustees signed a 20-year mortgage note in the amount of $214,000 to pay for the new classrooms. The actual cost of the construction was $248,760. The growing housing developments around the church and the increase in the size of the church building was the first step in transforming Haymarket Baptist from a small rural church to a growing suburban one.

One note of interest regarding the new addition was the impact it would have on the grave sites located on the Haymarket Baptist Church property. Due to earlier changes to the building, these graves were quite close to the structure. There was no way to do the proposed addition without disturbing the graves. There was much discussion among the church members as to how this could be handled. Two proposals were put forth. The graves could be moved, or the new addition could be built around the small cemetery. To honor their ancestors, the church body was adamant that the graves not be moved. Blueprints were drawn and construction was completed so that the four graves remained undisturbed. Haymarket Baptist now surrounds the family buried there.

To sustain the current membership and in an effort to increase it, the church deacons engaged in visitation prior to each deacon meeting. There was an effort to involve members of the church, but few were interested in this activity. The visitation, however, was successful. Many of the families who were visited did join the church. Unfortunately, scheduled visitation was dropped a few years later, despite its record of success.

There was also a large and active youth group at that time. They engaged in weekly Bible study, camping trips, week-long excursions to Virginia Beach, and fun daytrips to King's Dominion, ice skating, and outings to the movies. Even the fun activities were accompanied by Bible study. It was at this time that the youth took their first out of state mission trip. They traveled to Maryland for a week to help another church with their Vacation Bible School.

In September of 1988, a task group was appointed to study the possibility of opening a preschool to utilize the newly constructed classrooms. An offer was made to Louise Jamison, a church member who was already operating a preschool in the area, to move her business to the facility at Haymarket Baptist Church. She did not feel that the offer the church made to her was in her best interest, so it was declined. The church eventually located another director willing to take on the formidable task of starting a preschool. Haymarket Baptist Church Preschool was opened in 1989.

Rev. Lee, concerned about the controversy that was taking place in the Southern Baptist Convention (SBC) appointed a Denominational Sub Committee of Deacons that would follow the events happening in the Convention and keep Haymarket Baptist members informed. This struggle occurred between the conservatives and the moderates within the organization. The moderate segment had been in control of the SBC for many years, but in 1979, the conservative wing gained control. The disagreement was so strong that this action was referred to by the conservatives as a "Conservative Resurgence" but by the moderates as a "Fundamentalist Takeover."

Haymarket Baptist had always been a part of the Southern Baptist Convention, but the controversy then stirring in that organization was a source of worry for many of the congregants. The typically conservative church was beginning to move toward a more liberal approach to biblical exposition and societal mores. The church would carefully and cautiously watch the division in the Southern Baptist Convention and chart its course from the result.

A totally new activity brought to Haymarket Baptist by Rev. Lee was a shared community Thanksgiving Eve Service. Each year the location of this service rotated among four local churches: Haymarket Baptist, St. Paul's Episcopal, Mt. Pleasant Baptist, and Gainesville United Methodist. Whichever church hosted the service did not have to provide the speaker or the special music. Those activities were performed by one of the other churches. So the congregations might meet at Gainesville United Methodist, listen to Rev. Lee give the sermon, and enjoy the music of the Mt. Pleasant choir. This shared service crossed many lines between denominations. St. Paul's was the only Anglican church with the others being protestant denominations. Mt. Pleasant was an African American church; the others consisted of mostly Caucasian congregations. St. Paul's was the only church that used wine instead of grape juice for the communion cup. This caused a bit of interest among the youth members of Haymarket Baptist, and a lot of coughing after drinking!

Among the other new innovations started by Rev. Lee was the placement of a red rose in the sanctuary for a newborn baby in the church family. This flower was presented to the parents by their deacon at the conclusion of the service. This tradition continues today. Rev. Lee also began holding two services on Sunday morning, the first at 8:45 and the second at 11:00. Attendance was never great at the fist service, averaging 49. However, the effort was made in an attempt to grow the number of people attending the church.

Rev. Lee was also the first Haymarket Baptist pastor to hire an Associate Pastor to help with the needs of the church. Joel Wetherington was called in April of 1989 as the Minister of Youth and Education, a popular specialization at that time. He underwent an ordination examination by Potomac Baptist and was ordained in September 1989. On July 30, 1990, Rev. Wetherington tendered his resignation because he was returning to seminary to complete a doctoral degree. Records are missing to give the exact date, but he was replaced by Rev. Vicki Lumpkin as Minister of Youth and Education. She was the first female Associate Pastor employed by Haymarket Baptist.

There were two fires that destroyed some of the records of Haymarket Baptist. One was in the Haymarket Museum where official town documents were stored. These included building applications for additions to the church. Luckily, some members had detailed records that contained this information. The second fire was in the Pastor's office during Rev. Lee's tenure.

Many documents were lost, but no damage was done to the church because the fire was discovered quickly. One of the records that was lost in the fire was the date for the ordination of Mrs. Jane Strong, aka Miss Jane, Haymarket's first female deacon. The closest date that can be arrived at was that this also happened while Rev. Lee was pastor at Haymarket.

The hiring of Rev. Lumpkin, who had also sat for an ordination council with Potomac Baptist Association, and the ordination of Miss Jane as a deacon were both done during the continued struggle in the Southern Baptist Convention. While that organization had declared that the pastorate was to be a male-only position, Haymarket Baptist employed a female pastor and ordained a female deacon. This was an indication of the move away from conservatism that had been a foundational belief of the church.

Because opposition was anticipated, Miss Jane was carefully chosen to be the first female deacon in the church. She had attended Haymarket Baptist from early childhood. Her parents, Quentin and Pauline Lawler, were foundational members of the church. Though they had not been part of the group that separated from Antioch Baptist, they were early members of the church. Quentin Lawler joined Haymarket Baptist in 1925. His support of the church was so strong, and he was so loved, that when he passed away, the Sunday School class that he attended was named the Lawler Class in his honor. It bears that name to this day. With this background, it was rightly believed that no one would oppose Miss Jane as a deacon.

By 1990, 20 students were enrolled in the Preschool,

with 26 being the break-even number. The church was making payments on the debt incurred for the addition of the wings that now housed the preschool and supporting the preschool in its infancy. Unfortunately, these extra expenses meant that the church budget could not be met. Though attendance numbers were good, with the church averaging 140 in Sunday School, the budget crunch was worrisome. At this time, the Sunday evening worship was halted and replaced with occasional special studies. Another change in the budget at this point was defunding the Cooperative Program while maintaining gifts to both home and foreign missions through the Southern Baptist Convention network. This was another step toward separating from the Southern Baptist Convention and one more step away from the conservative roots of the church.

By 1992, the Preschool was doing well enough that it began to make payments to the church for the extra utility usage. Enrollment was growing each year. Average attendance for Worship service was 151 and for Sunday School was 141. The debt was being paid down by about $28,000 each year. Everything except the mission funding was paid. The church was doing well. Then things began to fall apart.

In May 1996, Rev. Lee submitted his resignation to Haymarket Baptist Church. He met with several of the church leaders and confessed that he was experiencing marital difficulties. He felt that under those circumstances it was best that he leave the church. His letter of resignation was read by a church member following the next Sunday morning worship service. A short time later, a Special Called Business Meeting was scheduled to discuss new developments in the resignation. Many of the church members felt that Rev. Lee should be allowed to remain in the church despite the personal issues that he was experiencing. They asked that the church vote that night to reject his resignation. However, it was pointed out that according to the church constitution, it was not up to the congregation to make that decision. The motion was ruled out of order. If Rev. Lee wished to remain as pastor, he would have to re-apply for the position. With that decision, the church split.

This was a horrific period for Haymarket Baptist Church. There had been disagreements at other times, but this was the first true schism in the church that resulted in members leaving and moving their membership. The ironic part of this is that they moved their membership to Antioch Baptist, reopening Haymarket's mother church. This was not a slow trickle of attrition. It was a mass exodus. The members remaining at Haymarket Baptist were devastated. They were without a pastor, and friends had withdrawn from the church. Haymarket Baptist was now truly a different church.

> It was a terrible time [when Rev. Lee left], worse than anything that happened at any of the other 15 churches where I've been a member.
>
> **Anonymous**

Without a pastor to lead the flock, more changes had to be made. Sunday services were cut to only one, and Sunday evening classes were stopped, Worship and Sunday School attendance plummeted to 102 and 70 respectively. The church immediately formed a pastor search committee to locate an interim pastor to lead the flock that found themselves without a shepherd.

Once again, in their time of need, God provided. Dr. Dallas Stallings accepted the call from Haymarket Baptist and started as interim pastor in July 1996, two months after Rev. Lee's resignation and sudden departure. Haymarket Baptist was completely shattered as the remaining members were stunned by both what they had learned about their pastor and the ensuing behavior of fellow members, who had left the church harboring strong negative feelings. In addition to the emotional upheaval, there was also a looming budgetary crisis. The loss of membership also meant a loss of income from offerings. Yet the bills still had to be paid. Even in circumstances such as these, the church would go on.

Dr. Stallings, with BA in Religion from Wake Forest University, a Bachelor of Divinity, Master of Theology, and Doctor of Ministry from Southeastern Baptist Theological Seminary, was the right man for the job. God chose well, as He always does! In his first meeting with the board of deacons, Dr. Stallings stressed the responsibility of the deacons for the church family, especially in a situation like the one they faced. He told them that they should encourage attendance and stewardship, two things that often drop when a church is without a pastor even under good circumstances. Deacons were encouraged to look at this time as a new beginning and to lead members to do the same. Rev. Lee had initiated a self-study and strategic plan before leaving (the second one in the church history); this would be a good time to evaluate and implement those ideas. Visitors should be encouraged and welcomed as if everything was normal. This focus epitomized Dr. Stallings approach to ministry. He was a caring person who was capable of looking to the future without losing sight of the immediate situation.

There was no doubt that Dr. Stallings had the ability to lead Haymarket Baptist through this troubled time. However, that does not mean that everything was perfect. He was very different from the previous pastors who had led Haymarket Baptist. He was the first pastor to hold a doctoral degree. Dr. Miller, a previous pastor, had also held a doctoral degree, but he was an interim. At this point, Dr. Stallings was also an interim. However, he would go on to become the full-time pastor of Haymarket Baptist. This made him the first pastor of the church with the title of Doctor.

A second difference was that he wore a ROBE! Some of the congregation were delighted with this attire. They felt that it added dignity and reverence to the sermon by pointing out the special calling of the preacher. Others were not supportive. They felt that it was too much like the dress of Catholic and Lutheran priests. Still others objected because it served to set the pastor apart as somehow different from or better than the congregation. This was antithetical to the Baptist tenet of the Priesthood of the Believer. This precept holds that an individual does not need an intercessor to go before God on his behalf. Baptists believe that each person can approach God him/herself.

There was also the belief that this bordered on a "high church" form of worship. This style of worship is typically associated with the Anglican/Episcopal tradition. It is a highly formal style of worship with the use of ritual, liturgy, and accoutrements in worship. Most Baptists adhere to a "low worship" style. This type of service lacks the structured ritual of high church and does not have the formalized use of accessories that are prevalent in high church. Low church services are typically evangelical in their topic and presentation. Haymarket Baptist moved closer to a high church form of worship under the leadership of Dr. Stallings. He had the Lord's Prayer printed in the bulletin, and it was recited by the congregation every Sunday. When administering communion, Dr. Stallings drank from a crystal goblet filled with grape juice. He raised this above his head for emphasis before drinking. To some this reeked of high church!

> **Haymarket Baptist Church and Broad Run Baptist Church were on the same church "field" as I was growing up and shared a minister.**
>
> **In 1950, at the age of 8, I accepted Christ, and when it came time to be baptized, Broad Run did not have a baptistry, so we came to Haymarket and used their baptistry. Believe it or not, it looks the same today as it did then!**
>
> **Through the years growing up, I became familiar with names at Haymarket like Lightner, Lawler, Robinson, Nichols, Thompsons.**
>
> **In 2003, as Raye and I walked into Haymarket Church, we were met by Tommy Robinson (whom I had not seen in years). He shouted out "Lord, child, what are you doing here?!!" his eyes twinkling and a big welcoming smile!!!**
>
> **Bernice Pearson**

In its present state of turmoil, some members were quite concerned about these behaviors. There was the beginning of a small schism over these additions to the worship. Despite this small disagreement, the church held together and moved forward.

At the beginning of his second year at Haymarket Baptist, Dr. Stallings sent a letter to the Deacons. This was another example of his caring and thoughtful leadership in the church. He began by stating that the church was "at the beginning of a new church year that is ripe with great possibilities and opportunities for growth and spiritual development." Just a year out from the disagreement that had so fractured the church, Dr. Stallings reminded the deacons, and thus the congregation through them, that the church must look ahead and move forward. In response to this, the Deacons set up a visitation program to follow up with visitors who came to the church. Sunday School attendance at Haymarket Baptist had dropped from an average attendance of 137 during Rev. Lee's last few years to only 95 in 1997. The Preschool was in its eighth year with 55 students enrolled. A Pastor Search Committee had been formed and it was beginning the task of locating a new full-time pastor to lead the church. Despite the financial constraints brought on by the loss of membership, Haymarket Baptist was still able to meet the payments on the mortgage, and all bills were being paid except the mission obligations. These were running behind once again.

At some point during Rev. Lee's tenure, and for no known reason, the Mission Committee had been dropped from the church Constitution. In January of 1998, under

Dr. Stallings guidance, the Mission Committee was returned to the Constitution. It was the responsibility of this committee to promote and encourage mission activity and awareness within the church. It is a strong Baptist belief that the purpose of a church is to spread the word of God to others. Despite the many transformations, Haymarket Baptist was returning to its roots. That year, 17 people joined the church. The efforts of the deacons and pastor were reaping a harvest for God. There was even a small budget surplus after all the bills, including the designated mission gifts, had been paid. There were 88 students enrolled in the Preschool. Things were growing at Haymarket Baptist!

The following year, 1999, was a red-letter year for Haymarket Baptist, bringing monumental changes. After two years of work, the Pastor Search Committee recommended to the church membership that Dr. Stallings be called as the full-time, permanent pastor of Haymarket Baptist Church. On May 23, 1999, there was a Service of Installation for Dr. Stallings. He officially became the pastor of Haymarket Baptist Church. This service was another new experience for this church. Other pastors had simply accepted the job offer and gone to work. For Dr. Stallings, there was an official ceremony with multiple readings and responses.

The following year was just as exciting. Recognizing that the money paid in interest on the mortgage could be better spent on mission activities, the church held a series of special offerings to raise funds to pay off the debt. In December of 2000, six years ahead of schedule, the last payment was made. Haymarket Baptist was debt-free!

On January 7, 2001, a special service was held featuring the burning of the note to celebrate the early retirement of the debt. As the debt was going down, attendance was going up. The average attendance in 2000 was 113, a great improvement over what it had been.

In 2004, Haymarket Baptist accomplished another first. The church had originally been a part of the Potomac Baptist Association. At that time, anyone wishing to seek ordination to the ministry did so through the Association. The examination would take place with a committee appointed by Association officers. In 2003, Potomac Baptist and Mt. Vernon Associations merged to form the NorthStar Church Network. NorthStar did not form ordination councils but left that up to the individual churches. John Carey, a member of Haymarket Baptist, sought ordination to the ministry. An ordination council was formed by Dr. Stallings to examine Mr. Carey's qualifications. He became the first minister to undergo examination and ordination at Haymarket Baptist Church. Also in 2004, Mission giving rose to 16.5% of total budget offerings. Out of approximately 1400 Baptist Churches in Virginia, Haymarket Baptest ranked 49th in mission giving.

The remainder of the time that Dr. Stallings spent at Haymarket Baptist passed tranquilly. The pain of the split in the church passed. The excitement of paying off the mortgage ebbed. The work of the church proceeded. A minister was ordained, and by 2005, average worship attendance had grown to 125. The members of the church had learned to persevere. On November 14, 2005, Dr. Stallings presented the church with his letter of resignation. He was ready to retire.

For the next year and a half, Haymarket Baptist Church was once again without a pastor. Even though there had been no crisis that lead to this situation, it is difficult for a church to function without an appointed leader. There is a feeling of unease in a congregation that is functioning without a pastor. When will we find a new pastor? *Will* we find a new pastor? What will he be like? What will happen to our church? During this period of uncertainty, Dr. James Vail, Chairman of the Board of Deacons, held the church together. One member of the church commented that Dr. Vail "sweated blood" through that time. Even though Baptist churches are run by congregational decisions and votes, a leader is still indispensable. Dr. Vail provided that guidance and sustained Haymarket Baptist. But a pastor was needed.

During this interim time, visiting preachers provided the Sunday morning sermon. Attendance numbers, surprisingly, held steady. It is typical that attendance drops when there is no pastor, even if it is just for a period of vacation. Budget numbers were good, not surprisingly. The Preschool became Haymarket Baptist Church Preschool and Kindergarten. Three classes of kindergarten were added to the school. Enrollment for these new classes was full from the beginning.

Finally, to the relief of the membership, Dr. Charles Stewart became pastor of Haymarket Baptist Church on April 1, 2007. Dr. Stewart earned a BA in Religion from Mercer University, a Master of Divinity from Southern Baptist Theological Seminary, and a Doctorate of Ministry from Baptist Theological Seminary. In addition to this, his wife, Amy, was also an ordained minister. She held a BA in Social Studies Education from Wake Forest and a Master of Divinity from Southern Baptist Theological Seminary. This was a new experience for Haymarket Baptist. Another welcome change with the Stewarts was that they were younger than any pastor and family since the Bradleys. When the Stewarts joined the church, their family included two sons, Carter, 11, and Harrison, 5. While they were at Haymarket Baptist, a third child, Madeline, was born.

Because there was no crisis within the church that brought Dr. Stewart to Haymarket Baptist, he was able to take the time to get to know the people of the congregation as he settled into the job. There was no immediate emergency from which the church needed to be rescued, so the transition was easier than it had been for previous pastors.

As with any change, there is always a period of adjustment. Because there was no dire need that brought Dr. Stewart to Haymarket Baptist, comparisons to Dr. Stallings were easily made. In some ways the two men were quite similar. Both wore robes during services, though Dr. Stewart accommodated that segment of the congregation who did not like them by wearing a robe for only half of the year. He also added an additional litany to the Sunday morning Service. At that time, Haymarket Baptist was an aging congregation. In an effort to attract younger members, Dr. Stewart added an acolyte section to the morning worship. During this, while the organ chimed the hour, two middle-school aged children would light the candles and open the Bible that sat on the altar table. The reason for this inclusion was valid. If the children had a "job" in the church, they would want to be in church. If the children wanted to attend, their families would also be there. Despite the legitimate reasons for instituting this into the service, this was another step toward the idea of "high church" behavior, taking one more step away from historical Baptist behavior.

Under Dr. Stewart's leadership, Haymarket Baptist moved even further away from the Southern Baptist Convention. In the intervening years since that organization was discussed at Haymarket, several things had occurred in associational bodies. The initial uproar over the reclaiming of the SBC by conservatives had eased. Out of that act, however, many other organizations had come into existence, vying with the SBC for member churches and their monetary support. When Haymarket Baptist began sending money to support missions, it was done through the Cooperative Program, the SBC branch that provides support for state conventions and missionaries. Haymarket Baptist stopped sending money to the Cooperative Program when Rev. Lee was pastor, choosing instead to give directly to the missionary support systems of the SBC.

The final act that tipped the scale away from the SBC at Haymarket Baptist was the insistence by the SBC, years earlier, that its missionaries agree with the Baptist Faith and Message statements. This document summarizes, based on biblical doctrine, what Southern Baptists believe about the Bible, the nature of God, and grace and salvation. The employment contracts of those missionaries who did not agree to teach and evangelize based on the beliefs put forth in the Baptist Faith and

Message were not renewed. It was that act that caused the SBC to basically be dropped from the vocabulary at Haymarket Baptist during the tenure of Dr. Stewart.

In previous years, members of Haymarket Baptist had participated in mission trips to both South Africa and Haiti. Over the years, however, such activities ceased to take place. This may have been due to the previously mentioned aging congregation. It could also be because the congregation began to focus more inwardly than externally. At one time, Haymarket Baptist contributed 25% if its budget to missions. In 2009, that number was 18%. Over the years that money dwindled. While Dr. Stewart was at Haymarket Baptist, funding for missions fell to 10% of the budget. It rose to 12% but was cut to 6.7% due to another period of budget short falls. Once the budget constraints were overcome, mission's contributions rose once again to 8% and then to 10%.

The one area of missions that was thriving was the relationship with HopeTree Family Services. Remember that Baptist Orphanage that Haymarket Baptist donated money to oh so long ago in 1917? The church continued its support through the years. An Annual Walk for Hope was started in 2011. Some members frequently drove to Salem where the campus is located to take supplies for the programs there. The Mission Committee even sponsored a trip for church members to visit the campus. Money collected during the Children's Sermon on Sunday morning is also sent to HopeTree, aka, the Baptist Orphanage of Virginia.

Haymarket Baptist Church Preschool and Kindergarten was thriving. In addition to the regular classes offered, extra activities were added such as a Lego club, fitness classes, and music. There was even a bug lady who visited on occasion. The police and fire department stopped by to talk with the children. There were also Parenting classes offered for adults. All these extra activities meant that the Preschool classes began to move outside the sections of the church that were designated for their use. This created some contention in the church as some members felt that the school was encroaching too much on "church areas." There were occasional conflicts when a member would arrive to conduct an activity only to discover that the room that was intended for that event was already occupied by a group of preschoolers.

As complaints began to be voiced more and more by some members of the church, Dr. Stewart interceded by calling in the director of another preschool to observe and study what was happening with the Haymarket Baptist school. At the conclusion of the observation period and meetings with the Preschool Director and Council, a meeting was held to discuss the findings. The guest who had observed the preschool was actually envious of many of the things done there. She told the gathered group that she intended to implement some of those things in the school that she ran. It would seem that hearing such a glowing report would have eased the angst among some of the church members. However, as Dr. Stewart called the meeting to order that night, he made the statement that it was "his meeting" and no one else was allowed to speak. This prevented those who were unhappy with the preschool from being able to voice their concerns in a public forum. Unfortunately, the meeting ended with attitudes toward the Preschool still sharply divided. Ironically the one bit of advice given by the guest was that there should be more communication between the church and the preshool.

On Wednesday evenings, Dr. Stewart led Bible studies in conjunction with Prayer Meeting. These sessions were engaging and well attended. There was usually a discussion of the scripture being studied and an application that was relevant for those in attendance. An interesting discussion rose one evening around Matthew 5:29. Dr. Stewart made the comment that Jesus did not really want you to pluck out your eye as the verse said. He asserted that was hyperbole. One member called him on that, questioning how one could tell what was true and what was hyperbole. This member stated that if the Bible is inerrant, then that verse was true.

Two other noteworthy events occurred while Dr. Stewart was pastor of Haymarket Baptist Church. Linda Garrett, a member of the church, sought ordination to the ministry. An Ordination Council was convened to meet with Dr. Garrett to determine her qualifications. She passed this examination and was ordained at Haymarket Baptist Church on February 2, 2008. Years earlier, Vicki Lumpkin had been ordained at this church, but this was done under the auspices of the Potomac Baptist Association. Linda Garrett was the first woman to undergo both the examination aspect by members of the church and be ordained at Haymarket Baptist Church.

The second major event that happened for Haymarket Baptist Church occurred in 2013. The Sanctuary had last been renovated in 1973. The passage of time and many feet had worn the carpet, and the padded seats bore the impressions of those who had sat there. At the vote of the church, the sanctuary was to be out of use for one week to remodel the interior. The pews were removed, the old carpet was ripped up, and the walls were painted. New red carpet was laid on the floor and the pews were reupholstered in red to match the carpet. The like-new pews were returned to the sanctuary. The wooden benches were removed from the choir loft and replaced with padded chairs to make seating arrangements more accommodating. The sanctuary gleamed like new once again.

In 2008, attendance at Haymarket Baptist began to drop. It had been 127 in 2007 but fell to 120 in 2008. This does not look like a major drop, but it was the beginning of a trend. By 2013, it had fallen to 107. Unfortunately, this was a phenomenon seen across America at that time. One reason for this is that Christianity was not seen as in vogue and there were too many other options. Religious freedom in America has certainly made it possible to choose from a plethora of belief systems. But it is not just religious choices that effect church attendance. Driving to church on Sunday morning, a person can see joggers on the footpaths, golfers teeing off, and shoppers on the way to the store. Religious connections are just not as important as they were years ago. According to Gallup polls, in 2008, 42% of people said that they attended church weekly. By 2017, that number had dropped to 38%.

In an effort to reverse this trend at Haymarket Baptist, Dr. Stewart held a series of meetings to brainstorm and discuss what could be done to draw more people to Haymarket Baptist. Lots of suggestions were given, but no decision was made as to what should be done. By 2015, the average attendance was down to 81.

On Easter Sunday, March 27, 1916, Dr. Stewart preached his last sermon at Haymarket Baptist Church. He had accepted a job offer to pastor a church in Marion, Virginia. The congregation bid him a fond farewell and prepared to be without a Senior Pastor once again.

~~~~~~

"THAT WAS AWFUL!" Lisa exclaimed. "I thought you said things got better!"

"They did. Weren't you listening when I told you about Dr. Stallings?" Mom said.

"Yeah. That part was good. And so was Dr. Stewart. But now he's gone!" Jeffery said.

"And so many people were upset about stuff like the Preschool and robes," Lisa said.

"But people get upset all the time," Dad answered.

"But they shouldn't do that in church," Jeffery protested.

"Maybe. But that's a good example that people who go to church are a lot like people who don't go to church. We're all imperfect sinners and need God to guide us and Jesus to save us."

"And if you were paying attention, you heard about two more Baptist distinctives," Mom prodded.

"I know," Lisa said eagerly. "Priesthood of the Believer."

"I was going to say that one!" Jeffery lamented. "Because I don't know what the second one was," he added.

"Me either," Lisa confessed. "I'm glad I said it first."

"The second one was the belief in the inerrancy of the Bible," Mom said. "Do you know what that word means?"

"No, I don't. And I bet Jeffery doesn't either," Lisa said.

"Hey! Wait a minute! Just because you don't know doesn't meant that I don't know," Jeffery said. "Too bad I don't know."

"It means that Baptists believe that all of the Bible is true. There are no mistakes," Dad said.

"So are you ready for more history?" Mom asked.

"How much more is there?" Jeffery asked. "I'm beginning to be sorry Lisa wanted to know all this."

"This was your question," Lisa exclaimed.

"There's only one more chapter in the history of Haymarket Baptist Church," Mom said.

~~~~~~

Chapter Notes

1. Eagle Eyrie is a conference and retreat center owned and operated by the Virginia Baptist Mission Board of the Baptist General Association of Virginia. It is located in the Blue Ridge Mountains near Lynchburg, VA

Sanctuary Following 2012 Renovation

Burning the Note, 2000
Pictured, left to right are:
Tommy Robinson, trustee
Dr. Dallas Stallings, Pastor
Joan Duckett, Trustee
Billy Swartz, Trustee
John Carey, Chair Board of Deacons

The Prospective Years

Unless the Lord builds the house,
The builders labor in vain.
Unless the LORD watches over the city,
The guards stand watch in vain.
Psalms 127:1

"Let's hear it then," Lisa said.

"Okay. I really do want to know about our church," Jeffery admitted.

~~~~~~

Haymarket Baptist was without a Senior Pastor again. This time the situation was different. They were without a *Senior* Pastor. The church now employed two pastors, so when Dr. Stewart resigned, the Associate Pastor could assume leadership until another Senior Pastor was hired. That Associate Pastor was Rev. Ruth Anne Sawyer. Rev. Sawyer had only recently been ordained after earning a Master's degree in Christian Ministry from the Rawlings School of Divinity at Liberty Baptist Theological Seminary. The departure of Dr. Stewart placed a heavy burden on a newly graduated and ordained minister. Dr. Stewart had accepted the position at Marion Baptist but delayed his departure from Haymarket Baptist to allow Rev. Sawyer time to adjust to her new position as Associate Pastor.

One advantage that Rev. Sawyer possessed was that she had been a member of Haymarket Baptist church for many years. She knew the people and the inner workings of the church. She had already served in many capacities in the church, including teaching in the Preschool, directing Vacation Bible School, and serving as a deacon. Now she stepped into the role of pastor, guiding the congregation through new changes, leading Bible studies, and conducting the Sunday morning worship.

Not everything that had to be done was related to worship and study activities. The newly renovated sanctuary seemed to highlight the worn appearance of other areas of the church. The carpet throughout the building was replaced in 2017. During this renovation the beautiful hardwood flooring of the staircases was revealed. Instead of covering these with carpet again, the wood was refinished and left showing. The following year the same procedure was done to the steps leading into the sanctuary.

A standard barometer for determining the health of a congregation is the attendance numbers.[1] When Dr. Stewart left, the average attendance was 81. By 2017, under the leadership of Rev. Sawyer, that number had risen to 105. Another indicator is the attitude of the people. Despite the concern of not having a Senior Pastor, there was a feeling of ease and happiness in the church. Rev. Sawyer was a capable leader and took charge of the running of the church. She continued in the tradition of both Dr. Stallings and Dr. Stewart in that she wore a robe in the pulpit, but she also created a less formal atmosphere for worship.

While all of these changes and renovations were taking place, a Pastor Search committee had been formed and was working to locate the next spiritual leader for Haymarket Baptist Church. A survey was distributed to the members of the church, seeking their input as to what they wanted in a new pastor. The old joke about Baptists is that if five of them get together, there will be at least eight opinions in the group. This was true of the results of the survey. There was very little consensus in what the congregation was seeking in a new leader. Finally, after an 18-month search, Haymarket Baptist Church chose Dr. Mark Olson as their Senior Pastor.

Dr. Olson came to Haymarket Baptist from the John Leland Center for Theological Studies where he had served as president. He had earned a B. A. at Wake Forest University, a Master of Divinity at Southern Baptist Theological Seminary, and Ph.D. in New Testament and Early Christianity from the University of Virginia. He was not a stranger to Haymarket Baptist because he had been one of the rotating preachers to fill the pulpit while the Search Committee was working. He had also preached once when Dr. Stewart was on vacation.

Dr. Olson immediately integrated himself into the church. He attended committee meetings, he visited people in the hospital, he learned everyone's names. To help him get to know his new congregation, he passed out an Individual and Family Information Questionnaire. The worship service became less formal under his leadership.

During the sermon, he actually engages the congregation by asking questions and expecting answers.

Haymarket Baptist Church Preschool and Kindergarten continues to thrive. Around 300 students are enrolled each year, and there is usually a waiting list to enter. They have expanded to offer additional activities both before and after school. The Rise and Shine Club is for children who need to be at school before regular classes begin, and the Cub Club is for those who need to stay later in the afternoon. Dr. Olson leads chapel for the children once each month. In 2019 HBCPK was named the Best Daycare Center and Preschool in the Haymarket Gainesville area. This is an award that they have won every year since 2014. Parents and children love the Preschool so much that they want it to add first grade classes. When the education wings were added, they were built in such a way as to allow the addition of a second floor if it was ever needed. Watch for future developments here!

Missions have been and remain an integral part of Haymarket Baptist church, by going, by giving, and by doing. Each year Haymarket Baptist participates in Operation Christmas Child. Every summer the youth go on a mission trip. The church has recently adopted the Robertson Boys' Cottage at Hope Tree Family Services. Church members will provide support for the boys staying there through birthday and Christmas gifts along with providing a gift for new arrivals. One member of the church currently serves on the Board of Trustees for HopeTree. The annual Walk for Hope is already scheduled. This fall, the Mission Committee is sponsoring a mission trip for members of the church. They will engage in doing carpentry work, teaching backyard Bible studies, and working in a food pantry. To this list can be added the Christmas Untrim a Tree, collections sent to areas ravaged by hurricanes, the ongoing food pantry and gas/motel cards for those in need, and the budgeted money for missionary support. Haymarket Baptist is living up to her missional roots.

> Children, Youth, Sunday School, worship, fellowship, committees, luncheons, dinners, Christmas programs before the Living Nativity. I always enjoyed the new member cookouts that we had in the early fall. That was a time of fellowship and really introducing yourself and your family. I have about 30 years of memories in this little white building called Haymarket Baptist Church.
>
> Dinah Thompson

Things are once again changing and growing at Haymarket Baptist Church. A new webpage was recently launched that will showcase the attributes of the church. The Wi-Fi system was upgraded to provide better coverage throughout the building. This is accessible to anyone at the church, members and guests. Sunday services are available on YouTube. Renovation continues with a kitchen "redo" that will bring the facility up to commercial standards. The Haymarket police determined that the bell in the steeple does not violate the noise ordinance, so the bell again peals on Sunday morning, announcing to all within hearing that God's people are gathering.

Attendance has remained steady since Dr. Olson's arrival, and new members with young children are coming to the church. One of the goals for the future that Haymarket Baptist has set for itself is to attract younger people to the church. They want to do this by being loving and friendly. They express this by having greeters at each door on Sunday morning. First time visitors are given a gift bag containing a pen with the church name and logo, brochures about the church, and seeds to be planted, illustrating the seeds that are planted by the people of Haymarket Baptist. There is also a "meet and great" at the beginning of the service that gives members the opportunity to speak with newcomers and old friends alike.

> The second week we visited this church my 5-year old son blurted out during the children's sermon 'I like this church way better than the other one!' While everyone in the sanctuary laughed, I realized we had finally found our 'home' church. This church has heart. This church is filled with love. This church sees you on Sunday and knows who you are. This church genuinely loves its members.
>
> Christy Wisor

There is currently a discussion regarding doing another self-study that will be used to develop a strategic long-range plan to guide Haymarket Baptist into the future. Part of the planning is to hire an Associate Pastor of Outreach. The search committee is already working to locate the person that God will send to them. The church is poised for the next phase of its life and ministry. They are making plans to grow and to plant seeds about the gospel news of Jesus the Christ.

Yet as they move forward, the past is not forgotten.

Haymarket Baptist is what it is today because of its past. Walking through the Haymarket Baptist Church building is a testimony of love. Around each corner, a memory lingers of someone who has gone before. Herb Young made the nativity that stands in the front yard of the church each Christmas. He led the crafts session of Vacation Bible School for many years. Samples of his crafts are on display in the church foyer. The tree in front of the church is the Tommy Tree, named for Tommy Robinson who cared for and loved this church for many, many years. This book is dedicated to his memory. Some people claim that his ghost lives in the attic. Pat McGahan made the display shelf above the copier. The food ministry is named Miss Jane's Pantry. We learned about her in a previous chapter. The first additions to the church were done by the members. Their spirits still fill the building. If you listen carefully, you can hear them whisper, "Love one another."

~~~~~~

"I GET IT NOW, MOM," Lisa whispered.

"Yeah me, too," Jeffery said.

"What do you get?" Dad asked.

"We go to this church because it's family," Lisa said.

"And they love everybody," Jeffery added.

"That's right," Mom said. "And sometimes, just like family, we get upset with one another, or we do things we shouldn't. But we are always family. Don't ever forget that."

~~~~~~

Chapter Notes

1. Throughout this book, attendance numbers have been used rather than enrollment numbers. The enrollment at Haymarket Baptist has been consistent over the years at around 300. Attendance, however, has fluctuated depending on what is happening in the church. This is typically true of all churches.

Postscript

THE FUTURE IS BECKONING Haymarket Baptist Church, and she looks forward to the coming years. The past has not always been easy. There has been turmoil and heartbreaks, disappointments and tragedies. But there has also been harmony and happiness, joy and triumph. The future probably will not always be easy either. But the people of Haymarket Baptist have learned much through their struggles that will aid them as they move forward. Over the years and through the difficulties, Haymarket Baptist learned to keep moving forward, to seek God's will, to stick together, to compromise where necessary but to always stand strong on biblical principles, and to love no matter what.

These are good lessons to take into the future. We truly stand on the shoulders of our ancestors, who may or may not have been giants. We see the results of their labors around us. Because of them, the small church that started with the courage of 28 people now has a membership of about 300 and a growing attendance. Each year 300 students fill the Preschool classes. Haymarket Baptist is a small but mighty church. None of this would be possible without the efforts of those who went before us. What legacy will we leave? In another hundred years, what will be recorded in the history of Haymarket Baptist Church? We all need to work together to make sure that it is worthy of our ancestors, and, especially, worthy of God.

Appendix A

People who left Antioch Church to start Haymarket Baptist Church

Crews Demory
Floyd Downs
Hollie Downs
Hattie Croson
Agnes Foley
Miss Elizabeth Foley
John W. Griffith
Mrs. J. W. Griffith
James P. Hulfish
Mrs. J. P. Hulfish
James A. Hulfish
Ruth Hulfish
W. W. Jordan
Alice Jordan
William D. Jordan
Daisy Jordan
Lillie Jordan

Mr. and Mrs. Will Jordon
Mrs. George Smith
Mildred Smith
Mrs. Sallie King
Alice Pickett
F. M. Smallwood
James R. Purcell
Mollie E. Purcell
Belle Smallwood
Mille Utterback
F. May Bragg

Appendix B

Haymarket Baptist Church Property Deed

Smith et al
To } Deed.
Trustees, Haymarket B. Church

This Deed, made and entered into on this the 1st day of November 1894, between George H. Smith and Mildred J. Smith, his wife, of Haymarket, Prince William County, Virginia, parties of the first part, C. M. White of Warrenton, Va., party of the second part, R. L. Payne of Fauquier Co. Va. Guardian of Mary L. Kelly, party of the third part, and George H. Smith, Wm. H. Jordan & G. E. Garnett, of Haymarket, Prince Wm. Co. Va. Trustees of Haymarket Baptist Church, parties of the fourth part. Witnesseth, that for and in consideration of the sum of ten dollars, the said George H. Smith and Mildred J. Smith, with general warranty, and the said C. M. White & R. L. Payne, with special warranty, have granted, bargained and sold and by these presents, do grant, bargain and sell, unto the said George H. Smith, Wm. H. Jordan & G. E. Garnett, Trustees for the Haymarket Baptist Church, all that certain tract or parcel of land lying and being situate in the Town of Haymarket, County of Prince William, and State of Virginia, on the North side of the Gainesville road, and bounded as follows, viz.: Beginning at a point in the centre of the said Gainesville road, and running S. 34½° E. 9 poles to stake No. 2, thence N. 55½° W. 5:1 poles to stake No. 3, thence S. 34½° W. 9 poles to stake No. 4, thence S. 55½° E. 5:1 poles to the beginning, and containing 45:9 square poles of land.

The said trustees and their successors are to hold said land in trust for the erection thereon of a Baptist Church building and necessary appurtenances, and for no other purpose whatever.

The said trustees and their successors are to hold said land in trust for the erection thereon of a Baptist Church building and necessary appurtenances, and for no other purpose whatever.

The said C. M. White, trustee and R. L. Payne, guardian as aforesaid do hereby release unto the said Wm. H. Jordan, Geo. H. Smith and G. E. Garnett trustees, all their interest, right and title, in said lot hereby conveyed, by reason of a certain deed of trust executed by said Geo. H. Smith & Mildred J. Smith, his wife to C. M. White, trustee, bearing date June 19th 1894, and recorded in Liber No. 43, f. 103 et seq., of the County Court Clerks Office of Prince Wm. Co. Va.

Witness the following signatures and seals.

G. H. Smith, (Seal,)
Mildred J. Smith, (Seal,)
C. M. White, Trustee, (Seal,)
R. L. Payne, (Seal,)
Gd'n for May L. Kelly

Prince William County, to wit:
I, Wm. F. Wharton a Justice of the Peace for the aforesaid County, State of

Appendix C

Pastors of Haymarket Baptist Church

1894-1904   C. W. "Wirt" Trainham
1904-1907   W. E. Lowe
1907-1910   J. A. T. Marsteller
1910-1914   T. D. D. Clark
1914-1915   Without Pastor
1915-1919   W. L. Naff
1919-1921   Edward Taber
1921-1922   Without Pastor
1922-1935   V. H. Council
1935-1936   M. C. Frazer
1936-1938   Without Pastor
1938-1950   J. Murray Taylor
1950-1952   Without Pastor
1952-1955   Robert L. Allen
1955-1956   Without Pastor
1956-1960   Edward H. Clarkson
1960-1962   Wayne E. Varner
1962-1967   Russell O. Cutchins
1967-1983   Walter L. Bradley
1983   Dr. Bruce Miller, Interim Pastor
1983-1996   Larry L. Lee
1996-2005   Dr. Dallas Stallings
2007-2016   Dr. Charles D. Stewart
2017-   Dr. Mark Olson

Appendix D:

Baptist Distinctives

The inerrant authority of the Bible.
The autonomy of the local church.
Believer's baptism of confessing adults by full immersion.
The Priesthood of the Believer.
Practice of only two ordinances: Baptism and the Lord's Supper.
The Separation of Church and State
Belief in only two offices within the governance structure of the church: pastors and deacons

Haymarket Baptist Church

Haymarket Baptist Church
July 1984

Old Fellowship Hall
Prior to last addition

Education Wing Construction

Haymarket Baptist Church 2019

2019 Kitchen Renovation

Haymarket Baptist Church Cemetery

Garnett Parents

Garnett Children

The Tommy Tree with Tommy Robinson
This tree replaced the original which was destroyed in a storm

Walter Bradley

Larry L. Lee

Dr. Dallas T. Stallings, Jr.

Dr. Charles Stewart

Dr. Mark Olson

About the Author

Dr. Edith Kennedy has been a member of Haymarket Baptist Church since she was a teenager. She holds five degrees, among them a doctoral degree in composition and rhetoric from George Mason University and a graduate certificate in biblical studies from New Orleans Baptist Theological Seminary. She has written numerous plays that have been performed at Haymarket Baptist, one of which has been published. She is also the author of the script for the Living Nativity that is produced every year. This past year, she created an Escape Room for the Youth that has already been requested by other churches.

When she is not writing, she spends time with her horses, claiming that her best ideas come when she is in the solitude of the barn. Without the distractions that occur at other places and times, she hears God's voice more clearly there.

www.ingramcontent.com/pod-product-compliance
Lightning Source LLC
Chambersburg PA
CBHW041313110526
44591CB00022B/2900